KNOWSLEY LIBRARY SERVICE

Please return this book on or before the date shown below

PROJECT LOAN

Let's look at
Food

Barbara Hunter

Heinemann
LIBRARY

Little Nippers

www.heinemann.co.uk/library
Visit our website to find out more information about **Heinemann Library** books.

To order:
☎ Phone 44 (0) 1865 888066
▤ Send a fax to 44 (0) 1865 314091
▭ Visit the Heinemann Bookshop at www.heinemann.co.uk/library to browse our catalogue and order online.

First published in Great Britain by Heinemann Library,
Halley Court, Jordan Hill, Oxford
OX2 8EJ, part of Harcourt Education.
Heinemann is a registered trademark of Harcourt Education Ltd.

Editorial: Jilly Attwood and Claire Throp
Design: Jo Hinton-Malivoire and bigtop, Bicester, UK
Models made by: Jo Brooker
Picture Research: Catherine Bevan
Production: Lorraine Warner

Originated by Dot Gradations
Printed and bound in China by South China Printing Company

ISBN 0 431 16384 7 (hardback)
06 05 04 03 02
10 9 8 7 6 5 4 3 2 1

ISBN 0 431 16389 8 (paperback)
06 05 04 03 02
10 9 8 7 6 5 4 3 2 1

British Library Cataloguing in Publication Data
Hunter, Barbara
Let's Look at Food
704.9'496413
A full catalogue record for this book is available from the British Library.

Acknowledgements
The publishers would like to thank the following for permission to reproduce photographs:
Agence Photographique de la Reunion des Musees Nationaux / © Succession Picasso/DACS 2002 p. **17**; AKG London pp. **4/5**, **6**, **8**, **22/23**; AKG London, © The Andy Warhol Foundation for the Visual Arts, Inc./ARS, NY and DACS, London 2002 p. **11**; Art Gallery of Ontario, Toronto, Canada/Bridgeman Art Library pp. **20/21**; Haags Gemeentesmuseum, Netherlands/ Bridgeman Art Library, © ADAGP, Paris and DACS, London 2002 p. **9**; Musee d'Orsay, Paris, France/ Bridgeman Art Library p. **10**; Musee d'Orsay, Paris, France/Lauros/Giraudon/ Bridgeman Art Library p. **7**; Private Collection/ Bridgeman Art Library p. **12**; Private Collection/Bridgeman Art Library, © ADAGP, Paris and DACS, London 2002 p. **13**; Private Collection/James Goodman Gallery, New York, USA/Bridgeman Art Library p. **18**; Private Collection/Portal Gallery Ltd/Bridgeman Art Library p. **19**; Chris Roberts-Antieau p. **16**; State Russian Museum, St. Petersburg, Russia/ Bridgeman Art Library pp. **14/15**.

Cover photograph reproduced with permission of The Art Archive / Museum of Modern Art Mexico / Dagli Orti.

The publishers would like to thank Annie Davy for her assistance in the preparation of this book.

Every effort has been made to contact copyright holders of any material reproduced in this book. Any omissions will be rectified in subsequent printings if notice is given to the publishers.

Contents

Food

In this book you will see photographs of how artists have painted or sculptured food.

Try to see how different they look to real food.

Prunkstilleben by Jans Davidsz Heem (1648)

Apples and oranges

Do you think this girl looks happy with her orange?

Child with Orange by Vincent van Gogh (1890)

6

The artist has used paint to make
this picture of apples and oranges.

Grapes

This fruit has been made out of stone. What do you think it would feel like to touch?

Basket of Fruit by Antonio Canova (1772)

This is an abstract painting. It doesn't look like the real thing. Can you find the grapes in this abstract painting?

Bananas

What colours are the bananas?

The Meal (The Bananas) by Paul Gauguin (1891)

Andy Warhol

The Velvet Underground and Nico (album) by Andy Warhol (1967)

Does this banana look real? This picture has been made by printing.

Melons

Viva la Vida by Frida Kahlo (1954)

Which of these melons
look the juiciest?

The artist has not painted the melons in this picture so carefully.

Still Life by Raoul Dufy (c. 1923)

Bread

Can you see any breadcrumbs in this picture?

Biscuits

Would you like to eat these biscuits?

Plate with Wafers by Pablo Picasso (1914)

16

Biscuits by Chris Roberts-Antieau

What is your
favourite kind
of biscuit?

Cakes

Many Happy Returns by Fernando Botero (1971)

Gateaux by Philip Le Bas (20th century)

How do these cakes look different?

Burger

Would you like to eat this giant burger?

The artist has made the burger from material and cardboard boxes.

Floor Burger by Claes Oldenburg (1962)

How many different types of fruit and vegetable can you see in this picture?

Autumn by Giuseppe Arcimboldo (16th century)

23

Index

The end

Notes for adults

This series covers the creative development area of learning. Each book looks at works of art from different cultures and different media. This set of books will support the young child's learning about the world around them and provide opportunities for them to explore different types of art. The following key Early Learning Goals are relevant to this series:
• explore colour, texture, shape, form and space in two or three dimensions
• respond in a variety of ways to what they see, hear, smell, touch and feel
• use their imagination in art and design.

Lets Look at Food includes different foods painted to appear life-like, abstract paintings of food, which look more like a pattern, and photos of 3-D sculptures from stone and paper.

Children will need to explore the differences between a 2-D painting and a 3-D sculpture. It will be necessary to explain that some artists represent their work in a literal way, like a photograph, while some paint or draw how an object 'feels' to them so it may not look like the 'real thing'. Discussing how some objects make children feel, or what they are reminded of when they see them, can help understanding.

Key vocabulary that can be explored through this book includes *painted, sculptured, colours, artist,* and also the many food names covered in the book, such as apples, grapes and bananas.

Follow-up activities
Children could look at, taste and touch the different food types suggested, and discuss the different textures and colours. The children could then represent what they see in different ways, using paint, pencils and plasticine or clay. They could also experiment using different food to print with and have fun discovering that foods with strong colours, such as red cabbage, can actually be used for colouring paper or material.